The Sa

GW01458811

The Sayings of

LEO
TOLSTOY

edited by
Robert Pearce

DUCKWORTH

First published in 1995 by
Gerald Duckworth & Co. Ltd.
The Old Piano Factory
48 Hoxton Square, London N1 6PB
Tel: 0171 729 5986
Fax: 0171 729 0015

A catalogue record for this book is available
from the British Library

ISBN 0 7156 2671 X

Typeset by Ray Davies
Printed in Great Britain by
Redwood Books Ltd., Trowbridge

Contents

Introduction

Leo Tolstoy (1828-1910) was a towering genius, a man of extraordinary creative energy. Whoever writes of his life, therefore, cannot avoid superlatives. According to Ernest Hemingway, Tolstoy 'could invent more with more insight and truth than anyone who has ever lived'. Another admirer has found in him 'perhaps the highest, most comprehensive, and most penetrating human intelligence to be found in any great creative writer anywhere'. The complete edition of his works, published by the Soviet government, totals no less than ninety large volumes, and among them are masterpieces of world literature. *War and Peace* is undoubtedly one of the greatest epic novels ever written, and *Anna Karenina*, a superbly realistic love story and much else besides, rivals it closely. But Tolstoy was not only a novelist. He was also a playwright, a short story writer, an educationalist, an essayist, a pamphleteer and a religious teacher. Maxim Gorky wrote that on his death, in 1910, the very world came to a halt.

Tolstoy's name will be forever linked with *War and Peace*, at once an intimate story of two families, the Rostovs and Bolkonskis, and an epic drama of the Napoleonic campaigns in Russia. Has a book ever contained such a magical mixture of the literary equivalent of close-up camera shots and wide-angled panoramic surveys? Never has there been such a complete picture of life. Tolstoy's technique is to introduce us to characters as we might meet them in real life: we obtain partial glimpses, and only get to know the whole person slowly and by degrees, as we might a friend. And many of the characters seem like friends. It has been said that Tolstoy saw all his characters, even the villains, with love. But *War and Peace* is not only a novel, and Tolstoy never referred to it as such: its 1,400 pages also include weighty historical and philosophical speculations. Yet few readers flag before the end, and many must have echoed George Orwell's only criticism of the book, that it does not go on long enough.

Tolstoy's fiction is unforgettable. Pierre, Natasha and Prince Andrei are indelibly fixed on the minds of his readers, as are Anna and Levin and dozens of 'lesser' characters (not caricatures complete with Dickensian catchphrases). Numberless scenes are vividly memorable: Orwell picked out the wolf hunt as the best thing in *War and Peace*; Malcolm Muggeridge believed that Natasha's visit to the huntsman's house was the best evocation of happiness in the whole of literature; and Hemingway judged the account of Bagration's rearguard action to be the finest relation of such a manoeuvre that he had ever read, better even than Tolstoy's Borodino. And who will ever forget the moving account of Andrei's last illness and his reconciliation with Natasha, or the terrifying evocation of Anna's paranoia before her suicide? The list is almost endless.

A turning point in Tolstoy's life came after the publication of *Anna Karenina* in 1877. Religion had always been a major influence, but now he underwent a thorough conversion, described in *A Confession*. Henceforth he devoted himself to trying to find the meaning of life; and that, to his mind, meant living simply and ascetically and trying to put into practice the precepts of the Sermon on the Mount, above all the injunction to 'resist not evil'. The cavalry officer who had served in the Crimean War became a pacifist and anarchist, the meat-eater a vegetarian, the wealthy aristocrat tried to adopt the lifestyle of a peasant, and the epicurean became a puritan castigating sex within, as well as outside, marriage. The novelist who had gloried in the inexhaustible variety of life now saw the need to teach people how they should live. A humanistic outlook gave way to a moralistic one.

Tolstoy, who had once described life, in the words of Shestov, as an 'enchanting ballroom', now pictured it as a 'torture chamber'. Critics howled. They wanted him to continue to write discursive novels (which to him had become 'abominations'), but instead they received denunciations of their sinfulness and homilies on reform. The critics have been howling ever since. Bertrand Russell believed that Tolstoy's theorising was worthless, and that it was the greatest misfortune for the human race that he had 'so little power of reasoning'. A recent biographer has commented that, after his conversion, Tolstoy began writing dreary books of 'half-baked religious thought'.

In fact Tolstoy continued to write works of remarkable quality and interest. His short stories now pointed simple morals, but Tolstoy did not disdain simplicity, believing that 'everything that is deep is transparently clear'. Some of these were undoubtedly great works of art. 'How Much Land Does A Man Need?' has been called the finest short story ever written, while *The Death of Ivan Ilyich* is often regarded as *the* great short novel in world literature. Certainly it must be considered among the most powerful and compelling accounts of a man's death ever written, while *The Kreutzer Sonata* is hypnotically charged with savage indignation. Even at his most didactic, Tolstoy was still an artist.

As for his overtly religious writings, they have had tremendous influence. Mahatma Gandhi considered them among the most important books he had ever read and called himself Tolstoy's 'humble follower', while the philosopher Wittgenstein found his interpretation of the gospels overwhelming. Few may believe that in old age

Tolstoy had found the absolute truth – his denunciations of Shakespeare and of women were too unbalanced for that – but many judge his later works to be among the most significant religious writings of the last two hundred years.

The authorities censored his books throughout his career, and in 1901 he was excommunicated. No doubt in a previous era he would have been crucified – and at least that would have silenced him. As it was, he exposed with total sincerity and devastating precision the corruptions and hypocrisy of organised religion. He also laid bare the inhumanity and moral bankruptcy of the Tsarist regime, for which he later received Lenin's tribute. Not that he approved of revolutionaries. When asked the difference between an 'execution' by the state and a 'murder' by a revolutionary, he replied there was a difference but that it was like that between cat and dog shit, and he did not like the smell of either.

'I can't understand why God chose such a repulsive creature as I through which to speak to people.' This diary entry shows Tolstoy's abject self-abnegation and, at the same time, his extreme arrogance. What he never achieved was humility, try as he might – and he did try, but a striving ego is an ego still. Tolstoy was a proud man with plenty to be proud about, given his literary achievements, and he was also a modest man with much to be modest about. But he was always, in some way, self-obsessed. His religious quest must be considered one of the most fascinating odysseys of modern man, and yet it brought him not peace but turmoil, culminating in his decision to leave his wife after forty-eight years of tempestuous marriage and in his subsequent death at the railway station in Astapovo. Yet Tolstoy undoubtedly loved the truth more than peace; and if God ever does speak through people, one wonders whether the author of the sublime 'Reply to the Synod's Edict of Excommunication' may not sometimes have been so inspired.

Tolstoy's life was a fascinating one, full of incident, paradox, monumental achievement and overpowering disappointment. He was soldier, aesthete, rake, holy man – and always a prolific writer of dazzling talents. He was, quite simply, a giant. Great as his works of literature are, they pale in comparison with his own life. He was himself his greatest character, and in his later years his estate, Yasnaya Polyana, became a place of worldwide pilgrimage.

All the phases of his titanic life are reflected in the sayings in this book. Tolstoy is not noted for his one-liners. The word 'Tolstoyan' conjures up images of epic profundity embodied in weighty tomes, and admittedly Tolstoy disdained provocative and witty, but at best half-true, Wildean epigrams. Indeed at times he could be prolix. But the following quotations show that he was a master of the sentence and paragraph as well as of the three-volume novel. He conveyed his vision of the world, its grandeur and simplicity, in microcosm as well as macrocosm – in sayings that are not glib but fathomless. Hence they require thought on the reader's part. How simple is the sentence: 'For the attainment of a good life it is necessary first of all to cease to live an evil life.' How easily the eye slides over the words. But Tolstoy takes his readers deeply – and harrowingly – into the meaning of a way of life which may seem civilised but which is built upon the suffering of others, until the words, like all his words, become pregnant with meaning.

R.D.P.

Sources

All quotations are taken from the works of Aylmer Maude, one of Tolstoy's first biographers and most faithful translators. In 1910 Tolstoy approved his translations, adding that 'I do not desire better ones'. Maude's Oxford Centenary Edition (1928-37) comprises twenty-one volumes, some prepared with the aid of his wife Louise. All the quotations below are identified by the relevant volume title.

Life of Tolstoy, 2 volumes, by Aylmer Maude

Translations by Aylmer and Louise Maude:
Childhood, Boyhood and Youth
Tales of Army Life
The Snow Storm and Other Stories
War and Peace
Anna Karenina
A Confession, the Gospel in Brief, and What I Believe
On Life and Essays on Religion
Twenty-Three Tales
What Then Must We Do?
Ivan Ilyich and Hadji Murad
The Kreutzer Sonata and Other Stories
Plays
What is Art? and Essays on Art
Resurrection
The Kingdom of God and Peace Essays
Recollections and Essays
Diary, 1847-57

War

Deep in each soul is a noble spark capable of making its possessor a hero, but it wearies of burning brightly – till a fateful moment comes when it will flash into flame and illumine great deeds.

Tales of Army Life

A soldier on the march is hemmed in and borne along by his regiment as much as a sailor is by his ship.

War and Peace, iii, 8

If man could find a state in which he felt that though idle he was fulfilling his duty, he would have found one of the conditions of man's primitive blessedness. And such a state of obligatory and irreproachable idleness is the lot of a whole class – the military. The chief attraction of military service has consisted and will consist in this compulsory and irreproachable idleness.

Ibid., vii, 1

War began, that is, an event took place opposed to human reason and to human nature. Millions of men perpetrated against one another such innumerable crimes, frauds, treacheries, thefts, forgeries, issues of false money, burglaries, incendiarisms, and murders, as in whole centuries are not recorded in the annals of all the law courts of the world, but which those who committed them did not at the time regard as being crimes.

Ibid., ix, 1

There is not, and cannot be, any science of war, and ... there can be no such thing as a military genius.

Ibid., ix, 11

Not only does a good army commander not need any special qualities, on the contrary he needs the absence of the highest and best human attributes – love, poetry, tenderness, and philosophic inquiring doubt. He should be limited, firmly convinced that what he is doing is very important (otherwise he will not have sufficient patience), and only then will he be a brave leader. God forbid that he should be humane, should love, or pity, or think of what is just and unjust.

Ibid.

The success of a military action depends ... on the man in the ranks who shouts 'We are lost!' or who shouts 'Hurrah!' And only in the ranks can one serve with assurance of being useful.

Ibid.

Men always lie when describing military exploits.

Ibid., ix, 12

At the approach of danger there are always two voices that speak with equal power in the human soul: one very reasonably tells a man to consider the nature of the danger and the means of escaping it; the other, still more reasonably, says that it is too depressing and painful to think of the danger since it is not in man's power to foresee everything and avert the general course of events, and it is therefore better to disregard what is painful till it comes, and to think about what is pleasant. In solitude a man generally listens to the first voice, but in society to the second.

Ibid., x, 17

War is like a game of chess ... but with this little difference, that in chess you may think over each move as long as you please and are not limited for time, and with this difference too, that a knight is always stronger than a pawn, and two pawns are always stronger than one, while in war a battalion is sometimes stronger than a division and sometimes weaker than a company.

Ibid., x, 25

The profoundest and most excellent dispositions and orders seem very bad, and every learned militarist criticizes them, when they relate to a battle that has been lost, and the very worst dispositions and orders seem very good, and serious people fill whole volumes to demonstrate their merits, when they relate to a battle that has been won.

Ibid., x, 29

A town captured by the enemy is like a maid who has lost her honour.

Ibid., xi, 10

Like a monkey which puts its paw into the narrow neck of a jug, and having seized a handful of nuts will not open its fist for fear of losing what it holds, and therefore perishes, the French when they left Moscow had inevitably to perish because they carried their loot with them, yet to abandon what they had taken was as impossible for them as it is for the monkey to open its paw and let go of its nuts.

Ibid., xi, 13

The strength of an army depends on its spirit.

Ibid., xiv, 2

She showed that alertness, that swiftness of reflection which comes out in men before a battle, in conflict, in the dangerous and decisive moments of life – those moments when a man shows once and for all his value, and that all his past has not been wasted but has been a preparation for these moments.

Anna Karenina

Love

To be beloved is a misfortune. It is a misfortune to feel guilty because you do not give something you cannot give. *Tales of Army Life*

I love her not with my mind or my imagination, but with my whole being. Loving her I feel myself to be an integral part of all God's joyous world. *Ibid.*

A youth in love trembles, is unnerved, and dare not utter the thoughts he has dreamt of for nights, but looks around for help or a chance of delay and flight when the longed-for moment comes.

War and Peace, iii, 13

If I were not myself, but the handsomest, cleverest, and best man in the world, and were free, I would this moment ask on my knees for your hand and your love!

Ibid., viii, 22

Ashamed as she was of acknowledging to herself that she had fallen in love with a man who would perhaps never love her, she comforted herself with the thought that no one would ever know it, and that she would not be to blame if, without ever speaking of it to any one, she continued to the end of her life to love the man with whom she had fallen in love for the first and last time in her life.

Ibid., x, 14

It is possible to love some one dear to you with human love, but an enemy can only be loved by divine love ... When loving with human love one may pass from love to hatred, but divine love cannot change. No, neither death nor anything else can destroy it. It is the very essence of the soul.

Ibid., xi, 15

To love everything and everybody and always to sacrifice oneself for love, meant not to love any one, not to live this earthly life. And the more imbued he became with that principle of love, the more he renounced life and the more completely he destroyed that dreadful barrier which – in the absence of love – stands between life and death.   *Ibid.*, xii, 4

All, everything that I understand, I understand only because I love. Everything is, everything exists, only because I love. Everything is united by it alone. Love is God, and to die means that I, a particle of love, shall return to the general and eternal source.

Ibid.

It is not beauty that endears, it's love that makes us see beauty.

Ibid., EP.I, 3

Levin was in love, and so it seemed to him that Kitty was so perfect in every respect, that she was a creature far above everything earthly; and he was a creature so low and so earthly, that it could not even be conceived that other people and she herself could regard him as worthy of her.

Anna Karenina

The more externally obedient and respectful his behaviour, the less in his heart he respected and loved her.   *Ibid.*

If so many men, so many minds, certainly so many hearts and kinds of love.

Ibid.

When his love had been stronger, he could, if he had greatly wished it, have torn that love out of his heart; but now, when it seemed to him that he no longer felt love for her, he knew that what bound him to her could not be broken.

Ibid.

Love those that hate you, but to love those one hates is impossible.
Ibid.

… that temporary beauty, which is only found in women during moments of love.
Ibid.

Respect was invented to cover the empty space where love should be.
Ibid.

Where love ends, there hate begins.
Ibid.

In the love between a man and a woman there always comes a moment when this love has reached its zenith – a moment when it is unconscious, unreasoning, and with nothing sensual about it.
Resurrection

Men live not by selfishness but by love.
Twenty-Three Tales

To love one person for a whole lifetime is like saying one candle will burn for a whole life.
The Kreutzer Sonata

Each time of life has its own kind of love.
Ibid.

The very best love is unconscious love.
Plays

One loves oneself not for what one is, but for what one appears to others to be.
Diary

Beauty one can get to know and fall in love with in an hour, then cease to love it just as quickly; but the soul one must learn to know.
Life of Tolstoy

It is a theory of mine that love consists in wishing to forget yourself, and therefore, like sleep, comes on most easily when you are dissatisfied with yourself or unhappy.

Ibid.

Only love unties every knot.

Ibid.

Never give way to the temptation of wanting people to love you.

Ibid.

Suffering & Death

Our good qualities do us more harm in life than our bad ones.

The Snow Storm

The best and greatest thing in life – to die without regret or fear.

Childhood

Intellectual work dries men up.

War and Peace, vi, 2

Man can be master of nothing while he fears death, but he who does not fear it possesses all.

Ibid., xi, 6

Death is an awakening.

Ibid., xii, 4

One can teach how many insects there are in the world and examine the spots on the sun and write novels and operas, without suffering; but to teach men their welfare, which lies in denying oneself and serving others, and express this teaching powerfully, is impossible without suffering.

Ibid., xiii, 3

When seeing a dying animal a man feels a sense of horror: substance similar to his own is perishing before his eyes. But when it is a beloved and intimate human being that is dying, besides this horror at the extinction of life there is a severance, a spiritual wound, which like a physical wound is sometimes fatal and sometimes heals, but always aches and shrinks at any external irritating touch.

Ibid., xv, 1

If we grumble at sickness, God won't grant us death.

Ibid.

One passes one's life finding distraction in hunting or in work, merely not to think of death.

Anna Karenina

There may be less charm in life when one thinks of death, but there's more peace.   *Ibid.*

He sought his former accustomed fear of death and did not find it. 'Where is it? What death?' There was no fear because there was no death.

Ivan Ilyich and Hadji Murad

In town a man can live for a hundred years without noticing that he has long been dead and has rotted away.

The Kreutzer Sonata

There is nothing in life. Death is the only real thing, and death ought not to exist.

Ibid.

Happy is he who has not been born: death is better than life, and one must free oneself from life.

A Confession

What are we who are convinced of the necessity of suicide yet do not decide to commit it, but the weakest, most inconsistent, and to put it plainly, the stupidest of men, fussing about with our own stupidity as a fool fusses about with a painted hussy?

Ibid.

At times when one's spirit sinks one must treat oneself as an invalid – and keep quiet!

Recollections and Essays

We are all sentenced to death and our execution is only deferred.

What Is Art?

When suffering is recognized and understood, it is redeemed.

Ibid.

When one suffers, it is necessary to enter into oneself, not to seek some external diversion which can only prevent one from seeing one's true self. When one comes back to oneself, everything becomes clear, and sufferings such as are not physical cease.

Diary

Suffering is not an evil which you must be rid of, but the work of your life which you must accept. In wishing to evade your suffering, you resemble a man who fails to push the plough where the ground is hardest.

Ibid.

The more we grow used to what is pleasant and refined in life, the more deprivations we store up for ourselves.

Ibid.

If you don't regard your life as a mission, then there is no life but only hell.

Life of Tolstoy

Death is the only place we can really go away to.

Ibid.

History & Causation

In historic events the so-called great men are labels giving names to events, and like labels they have but the smallest connexion with the event itself.

War and Peace, ix, 1

Man lives consciously for himself, but is an unconscious instrument in the attainment of the historic, universal aims of humanity.   *Ibid.*

A king is history's slave.   *Ibid.*

When an apple has ripened and falls, why does it fall? Because of its attraction to the earth, because its stalk withers, because it is dried by the sun, because it grows heavier, because the wind shakes it, or because the boy standing below wants to eat it?   *Ibid.*

Fortune is frankly a courtesan.   *Ibid.,* x, 29

To speak of what would have happened had Napoleon sent his Guards is like talking of what would happen if autumn became spring. It could not be.

Ibid., x, 34

To study the laws of history we must completely change the subject of our observation, must leave aside kings, ministers, and generals, and study the common, infinitesimally small elements by which the masses are moved. No one can say in how far it is possible for man to advance in this way towards an understanding of the laws of history; but it is evident that only along that path does the possibility of discovering the laws of history lie; and that as yet not a millionth part as much mental effort has been applied in this direction by historians as has been devoted to describing the actions of various kings, commanders, and minsters.   *Ibid.,* xi, 1

He who plays a part in an historic event never understands its significance.

Ibid., xii, 2

Man's mind cannot grasp the causes of events in their completeness, but the desire to find those causes is implanted in man's soul.   *Ibid.*, xiii, 1

If in the descriptions given by historians ... we find their wars and battles carried out in accordance with previously formed plans, the only conclusion to be drawn is that those descriptions are false.

Ibid.

When actions are clearly contrary to all that humanity calls right or even just, the historians produce a saving conception of 'greatness'. 'Greatness', it seems, excludes the standards of right and wrong. For the 'great' man nothing is wrong; there is no atrocity for which a 'great' man can be blamed.

Ibid., xiv, 4

The words *chance* and *genius* do not denote any really existing thing and therefore cannot be defined. Those words only denote a certain stage of understanding of phenomena.   *Ibid.*, EP.I, 1

The conception of the action of a man subject solely to the law of inevitability, without any element of freedom, is just as impossible as the conception of a man's completely free action.

Ibid., EP.I, 4

If the will of every man were free, that is, if each man could act as he pleased, all history would be a series of disconnected accidents.

Ibid., EP.II

The farther back in history the object of our observation lies, the more doubtful does the free will of those concerned in the event become, and the more manifest the law of inevitability.

Ibid.

Life in the past and in the future conceals from men the true life of the present.

A Confession

If a biography is to be written the whole real truth must be told. Only a biography of that kind – however ashamed one may be to write it – can be of any real benefit to its readers.

Recollections and Essays

Human Nature

Who is capable, even for a moment, of severing himself so completely from life as to look down on it with complete detachment?

The Snow Storm

Old age is sometimes majestic, sometimes ugly, and sometimes pathetic. But old age can be both ugly and majestic. *Ibid.*

Even in the best, most friendly and simplest relations of life, praise and commendation are essential, just as grease is necessary to wheels that they may run smoothly.

War and Peace, i, 2

We cannot renew an illusion we have once seen through.

Ibid., iii, 1

It is very difficult to tell the truth, and young people are rarely capable of it.

Ibid., iii, 6

From her smiling lips flowed sounds which one may produce at the same intervals and hold for the same duration, but which leave you cold a thousand times and the thousand and first time thrill you and make you weep.

Ibid., iv, 14

All we can know is that we know nothing. And that's the height of human wisdom.

Ibid., v, 1

If there were no suffering man would not know his limitations, would not know himself.

Ibid., xi, 6

A sweating hand's an open hand, a dry hand's closed.

Ibid., xiii, 3

A superfluity of the comforts of life destroys all joy in satisfying one's needs, while great freedom in the choice of occupation ... is just what makes that choice of occupation insolubly difficult, and destroys the desire and possibility of having an occupation.

Ibid.

One must have the prospect of a promised land to have the strength to move.

Ibid., xiii, 4

The power man has of transferring his attention from one thing to another is like the safety-valve of a boiler that allows superfluous steam to blow off when the pressure exceeds a certain limit.

Ibid., xiv, 3

Pure and complete sorrow is as impossible as pure and complete joy.

Ibid., xv, 1

If we admit that human life can be ruled by reason, the possibility of life is destroyed.

Ibid., EP.I, 1

There is no subject so trivial that it will not grow to infinite proportions if one's entire attention is devoted to it.

Ibid., EP.I, 3

Ideas that have great results are always simple ones.

Ibid., EP.I, 4

Nothing is so insufferable to man as to be completely at rest, without passions, without diversion, without study.

Anna Karenina

I am neither young nor old enough to find amusement in playthings.

Ibid.

One may sit for several hours at a stretch with one's legs crossed in the same position, if one knows that there's nothing to prevent one changing that position; but if a man knows that he must remain sitting with crossed legs, then cramps come on, the legs begin to twitch and to strain towards the new spot to which one would like to draw them.

Ibid.

One's not dull by oneself.

Ibid.

There was no solution but that universal solution which life gives to all questions, even the most complex and insoluble. That answer is: one must live in the needs of the day – that is, forget oneself.

Ibid.

No one is satisfied with his fortune, and everyone is satisfied with his wit.

Ibid.

Ennui – a desire for desires.

Ibid.

The aim of civilization – to make everything a source of enjoyment.

Ibid.

In infinite time, in infinite matter, in infinite space, is formed a bubble-organism, and that bubble lasts a while and bursts, and that bubble is me.

Ibid.

There are no conditions to which a man cannot become accustomed, especially if he sees that all around him are living in the same way.

Ibid.

The first drink sticks in the throat, the second flies down like a hawk, but after the third they're like tiny little birds.

Ibid.

The more he did nothing, the less time he had to do anything. *Ibid.*

One of the most widespread superstitions is that every man has his own special definite qualities: that he is kind, cruel, wise, stupid, energetic, apathetic, and so on. Men are not like that. We may say of a man that he is more often kind than cruel, more often wise than stupid, more often energetic than apathetic, or the reverse; but it would not be true to say of one man that he is kind and wise, of another that he is bad and stupid. And yet we always classify mankind in this way. And this is false. Men are like rivers: the water is the same in one and all; but every river is more narrow here, more rapid there, here slower, here broader, now clear, now dull, now cold, now warm. It is the same with men. Every man bears in himself the germs of every human quality; but sometimes one quality manifests itself, sometimes another, and the man often becomes unlike himself, while still remaining the same man.

Resurrection

It is generally supposed that conservatives are usually old people, and that those in favour of change are the young. That is not quite correct. Usually conservatives are young people: those who want to live but do not think about how to live, and have not time to think, and therefore take as a model for themselves a way of life that they have seen. *Ibid.*

All of us ... must have personal experience of all the nonsense of life, in order to get back to life itself; the evidence of other people is no good.

Ibid.

It is a bad thing not to be able to stand solitude.

Ibid.

I am always with myself, and it is I who am my tormentor.

Ivan Ilyich and Hadji Murad

When awake one can deceive oneself, but a dream gives a true valuation of the state one has attained to.

Ibid.

In all harmful things there is some good. After a conflagration we can warm ourselves and light our pipes from the glowing charcoal; but why say that the conflagration is useful? *Ibid.*

Man never has lived, and cannot live, without a philosophy of life. *A Confession*

Everyone struggles with his whole strength to obtain what he does not need.

Ibid.

Reason enforces nothing, it only sheds light.

Ibid.

There is no bad odour, no sound, no monstrosity, to which man cannot become so accustomed that he ceases to remark what would strike a man unaccustomed to it.

Ibid.

From a five-year-old boy to me is only a step, from a new-born babe to a five-year-old boy there is an immense distance, from an embryo to a new-born babe there is an enormous chasm, while between non-existence and an embryo there is not merely a chasm but incomprehensibility.

Ibid.

Why do people wish to stupefy themselves?

Ibid.

The man living in society finds solitude as beneficial as the man not living in society finds social intercourse.

Diary

There is a sort of sombre delight in despising people.

Ibid.

People learn to fly, instead of learning how to live a loving life ... It is as if birds were to stop flying and learn to ride bicycles.

Ibid.

Do not fear: nothing human is harmful to man. Do you doubt yourself? Surrender to the feeling and it will not deceive you.

Life of Tolstoy

We dislike people not because they are evil: we think they are evil because we dislike them.

Ibid.

Happiness & Pleasure

Forced merriment is worse even than boredom.

The Snow Storm

The desire for happiness is innate in every man.

Tales of Army Life

The only way to be happy is to love, to love
self-denyingly, to love everybody and everything; to
spread a web of love on all sides and to take all who
come into it.   *Ibid.*

One must believe in the possibility of happiness in order
to be happy.   *War and Peace*, vi, 12

The absence of suffering, the satisfaction of one's needs,
and consequent freedom in the choice of one's
occupation, that is, of one's way of life, now seemed to
Pierre to be indubitably man's highest happiness.

Ibid., xiii, 3

Man is created for happiness, happiness is within him, in
the satisfaction of simple human needs, and all
unhappiness arises not from privation but from
superfluity.   *Ibid.*, xiv, 3

He had learned that, as there is no condition in which
man can be happy and entirely free, so there is no
condition in which he need be unhappy and not free. He
learned that suffering and freedom have their limits and
that those limits are very near together; that a person in
a bed of roses with one crumpled petal suffered as
keenly as he now, sleeping on the bare damp earth with
one side growing chilled while the other was warming;
and that when he had put on tight dancing-shoes he had
suffered just as he did now when he walked with bare
feet that were covered with sores.   *Ibid.*

A cigar is ... not exactly a pleasure, but the crown and outward sign of pleasure.

Anna Karenina

She realised that one has but to forget oneself and love others, and one will be calm, happy, and noble.

Ibid.

Happiness lies in the search for truth, not in finding it.

Ibid.

The pleasures connected with his work were pleasures of ambition; his social pleasures were those of vanity; but his greatest pleasure was playing bridge.

Ivan Ilyich and Hadji Murad

The only certain happiness in life is to live for others.

The Kreutzer Sonata

The enjoyment of nature is the purest form of enjoyment.

A Confession

True happiness is always quiet and unnoticed.

Recollections and Essays

A man who lives for himself and his passions, however beautiful his wife may be and however distinguished and rich he becomes, cannot be happy.

What Is Art?

The best way to be happy is, without any rules, to throw out from oneself on all sides, like a spider, an adhesive web of love to catch in it all that comes: an old woman, a child, a girl, or a policeman.   *Diary*

No, this world is not a joke, and not a vale of trials or a transition to a better, everlasting world, but this world here is one of the eternal worlds that is beautiful, joyous, which we can and must make more beautiful and more joyous for those living with us and for those who will live in it after us.   *Ibid.*

Doctors & Teachers

'Dare to do and err' refers not so much to poets as to doctors and veterinary surgeons.

The Snow Storm

I was ill, and they tormented me and maimed me – doctoring me, as people call it.   *Ibid.*

In the country, people rarely try to educate their children and therefore unwittingly usually give them an excellent education.   *Ibid.*

What can doctors cure? One can't cure anything. Our body is a machine for living. It is organized for that, it is its nature. Let life go on in it unhindered and let it defend itself, it will do more than if you paralyse it by encumbering it with remedies. Our body is like a perfect watch that should go for a certain time.

War and Peace, x, 24

Physical and spiritual wounds alike can heal completely only as the result of a vital force from within.

Ibid., xv, 1

He had what the doctors termed 'bilious fever'. But despite the fact that the doctors treated him, bled him, and gave him medicines to drink – he recovered.

Ibid., xv, 5

That most powerful engine of ignorance, the diffusion of printed matter ...

Ibid., EP.II

He considered it his duty as a doctor to pose as a man whose every moment was of value to suffering humanity.

Ibid.

I have reached the extraordinary truth that man has eyes in order to see with them, ears in order to hear with them, legs in order to walk with them, and hands and a back to work with, and that if he does not use them for their natural purpose it will be the worse for him.

What Then Shall We Do?

If education is good, then the need for it will manifest itself like hunger.

Life of Tolstoy

Religion & Morality

If only man ... understood that every thought is both false and true!   *The Snow Storm*

God has made everything for the joy of man. There is no sin in any of it.   *Tales of Army Life*

A man is never such an egoist as at moments of spiritual ecstasy. At such times it seems to him that there is nothing on earth more splendid and interesting than himself.   *Ibid.*

What is bad? What is good? What should one love and what hate? What does one live for? And what am I? What is life, and what is death? What Power governs it all? ... The answer was: 'You'll die and all will end. You'll die and know all, or cease asking.'
War and Peace, v, 1

The highest wisdom is one. The highest wisdom has but one science – the science of the whole – the science explaining the whole creation and man's place in it.
Ibid., v, 2

Men always did and always will err, and in nothing more than in what they consider right and wrong.
Ibid., v, 9

Simplicity is submission to the will of God.
Ibid., xi, 6

Lay me down like a stone, O God, and raise me up like a loaf.   *Ibid.,* xii, 3

There is no greatness where simplicity, goodness, and truth are absent.
Ibid., xiv, 5

As the sun and each atom of ether is a sphere complete
in itself, and yet at the same time only a part of a whole
too immense for man to comprehend, so each individual
bears within himself his own aims and yet bears them to
serve a general purpose incomprehensible to man.

Ibid., EP.I, 1

Countess Mary's soul always strove towards the infinite,
the eternal, and the absolute, and could therefore never
be at peace.

Ibid., EP.I, 4

All he wanted now was to be better than before.

Anna Karenina

To put himself in thought and feeling in another
person's place was a spiritual exercise not natural to
Alexey Alexandrovitch. He looked on this spiritual
exercise as a harmful and dangerous abuse of the fancy.

Ibid.

It is better when one does good so that you may ask
everyone and no one knows.

Ibid.

The longer Levin mowed, the oftener he felt the
moments of unconsciousness in which it seemed not his
hands that swung the scythe, but the scythe mowing of
itself, a body full of life and consciousness of its own,
and as though by magic, without thinking of it, the work
turned out regular and well-finished by itself. These
were the most blissful moments.

Ibid.

Those joys were so small that they passed unnoticed,
like gold in sand, and at bad moments she could see
nothing but the pain, nothing but sand; but there were
gold moments too, when she saw nothing but joy,
nothing but gold.

Ibid.

Hypocrisy in anything whatever may deceive the cleverest and most penetrating man, but the least wide-awake child recognises it, and is revolted by it, however ingeniously it may be disguised.   *Ibid.*

I shall still dispute in the same way, shall express my thoughts inopportunely ... But my life, my whole life, independently of anything that may happen to me, is every moment no longer meaningless as it was before, but has an unquestionable meaning of goodness with which I have the power to invest it.   *Ibid.*

In former days the free-thinker was a man who had been brought up in ideas of religion, law, and morality, and only through conflict and struggle came to free-thought; but now there has sprung up a new type of born free-thinker who grows up without ever having heard of the principles of morality or religion.   *Ibid.*

If goodness has causes, it is not goodness; if it has effects, a reward, it is not goodness either. So goodness is outside the chain of cause and effect.   *Ibid.*

We shall be judged by our consciences and by God, not for the results of our deeds, but for our intentions.
Resurrection

Are you really acting according to your conscience, or are you doing it simply in order to show off?   *Ibid.*

It occurred to him that what had appeared perfectly impossible before, namely that he had not spent his life as he should have done, might after all be true.
Ivan Ilyich and Hadji Murad

The less importance he attached to the opinion of men the more did he feel the presence of God within him.
The Kreutzer Sonata

If life has no aim, if life is given us for life's sake, there is no reason for living.   *Ibid.*

It really is amazing how complete is the delusion that beauty is goodness.   *Ibid.*

The distance you have gone is less important than the direction in which you are going.
What Then Must We Do?

The very worst, most downright and deceptive lie to others is as nothing in its consequences compared with that lie to ourselves on which we have built our whole life.   *Ibid.*

The whole life of man with all its complex and diverse activities ... has no other purpose than the ever greater elucidation, confirmation, simplification, and diffusion, of moral truth.   *Ibid.*

There was reason for Christ to die on the cross: the sacrifice of suffering conquers all.   *Ibid.*

Only those to whom moral truths are serious and precious know how important and valuable they are, and by what prolonged efforts the simplification and elucidation of moral truth is reached.   *Ibid.*

To change another man's outlook one must oneself have a better one and live in accord with it.   *Ibid.*

One need only read the Prayer-Book and follow the ritual which is continually performed by the Orthodox priests and is considered a Christian worship of God, to see that all these ceremonies are nothing but different kinds of sorcery adapted to all the incidents of life.
On Life and Essays on Religion

Were Christ to come now and see what is done in his name in church, he would surely with yet greater and most just anger throw out all those horrible alter-cloths, lances, crosses, cups and candles and icons and all the things wherewith the priests – carrying on their sorcery – hide God and his truth from mankind.   *Ibid.*

God requires nothing but the truth.   *Ibid.*

There are two Gods. There is the God that people generally believe in – a God who *has to serve* them (sometimes in very refined ways, say, by merely giving them peace of mind). This God does not exist. But the God whom people forget – the God *whom we all have to serve* – exists and is the prime cause of our existence and of all that we perceive.   *A Confession*

God is that whole of which we acknowledge ourselves to be a part: to a materialist – matter; to an individualist – a magnified, non-natural man; to an idealist – his ideal, Love.   *Ibid.*

How is it that these gentlemen [priests] do not understand that even in the face of death, two and two still make four?   *Ibid.*

Faith is the strength of life … Only in faith can we find for life a meaning, a meaning not destroyed by sufferings, deprivations or death.

                    Ibid.

Every true doctrine is a dream to those in error.

                    Ibid.

Live seeking God, and then you will not live without God.   *Ibid.*

It was and is quite impossible to judge by a man's life and conduct whether he is a believer or not.

                    Ibid.

In the infinite there is neither complex nor simple, neither forward nor backwards, nor better or worse.

                    Ibid.

To say of any particular twig that it is the only true twig would be absurd. Yet that is just what is said by the Churches.   *Ibid.*

It is what lies at the basis of all the faiths that alone is true.

Ibid.

Real faith results from the inevitability and truth of a revelation that fully satisfies reason.

Ibid.

To study the faith of the Jews in order to understand the Christian faith is like studying a candle before it is lit, in order to understand the significance of the light which comes from a burning candle.

Ibid.

The Book of Revelation reveals absolutely nothing.

Ibid.

If God came down to earth to reveal truth to men, at least he would have revealed it so that all might understand: if he did not do that he was not God; and if the divine truths are such that even God could not make them intelligible to mankind, men certainly cannot do so.

Ibid.

Nothing more arrogant can be said than that the words spoken by me are uttered through me by God.

Ibid.

Not all can be initiated into the deepest mysteries of dogmatics, homiletics, patristics, liturgics, hermeneutics, apologetics, etc; but all may and should understand what Christ said to all the millions of simple, unlearned people who have lived and are living.

Ibid.

As fire does not extinguish fire, so evil cannot extinguish evil. Only goodness, meeting evil and not infected by it, conquers evil. That this is so is in man's spiritual world an immutable law comparable to the law of Galileo.

Ibid.

If the Gospels had been discovered half-burnt or obliterated it would have been easier to recover their meaning than it is now, when dishonest interpretations have been applied to them with the direct purpose of perverting and hiding the meaning of the teaching.

Ibid.

A man who has understood that he is really sinking cannot but catch at the rope of salvation.

Ibid.

All that is alive is independent of the Church.

Ibid.

In this demand for credulous belief in the impossible and unnatural we have reached such a pass that the very irrationality of that for which we demand credulous belief is considered a sign of its validity.

Ibid.

Religion – the very thing that gives man true happiness – is, in its perverted form, the chief source of man's sufferings.   *Recollections and Essays*

To replace what is earthly and temporary by what is eternal is the way of life, and along it we must travel.

Ibid.

The greater part of what is called religion is simply the superstition of past ages.   *Ibid.*

If work be not actually a vice, it can from no point be considered a virtue.

Ibid.

For the attainment of a good life it is necessary first of all to cease to live an evil life.

Ibid.

There never has been and cannot be a good life without self-control.   *Ibid.*

The temptation to win human praise that mingles with good actions is so harmful and so unavoidable that one must sympathize with efforts to avoid praise and even to evoke contempt.   *Ibid.*

Bereft of religion, men possessing power over the forces of nature are like children to whom gunpowder or explosive gas has been given as a plaything.

Ibid.

The cause of the world-wide consumption of hashish, opium, wine, and tobacco, lies not in the taste, nor in any pleasure, recreation, or mirth they afford, but simply in man's need to hide from himself the demands of conscience.   *Ibid.*

It is commonly said that reality is that which exists, or that only what exists is real. Just the contrary is the case: true reality, that which we really know, is what has never existed. The ideal is the only thing we know with certainty, and it has never existed.

Ibid.

Those who with their whole heart and with suffering seek God are already serving Him.

What Is Art?

The whole truth can never be immoral.   *Ibid.*

The man whose aim in life is his own happiness is bad: he whose aim is the good opinion of others is weak: he whose aim is the happiness of others is virtuous: but he whose aim is God is great.

Diary

It is easier to write ten volumes of philosophy than to put a single precept into practice.   *Ibid.*

Conscience is our best and most reliable guide ... But vanity speaks with equal force.

Ibid.

If we wait for the circumstances in which we can easily be virtuous and happy, we shall wait for ever.

Ibid.

Refrain from wine and women. The pleasure is so little and so indistinct, but the remorse is so strong.

Ibid.

To keep oneself totally apart in order not to become sullied is the most sullied thing of all.

Ibid.

If you want to break up a stone it is unfortunate that it is hard, but if you need a stone to sharpen something, then the harder, the better. It is the same with what are called sorrows.

Ibid.

Remorse is like the cracking of an egg shell or a grain of corn, as a result of which the seed starts to grow.

Life of Tolstoy

People don't obey God, they merely worship him. Better not to worship but to obey.

Ibid.

Men, Women & Family Life

Anna Fedorovna ... was already so far from young that she did not even consider herself young, which means a good deal for a woman. *The Snow Storm*

Men strive in life not to do what they think right, but to call as many things as possible *their own*. *Ibid.*

As is always the case with a thoroughly attractive woman, her defect ... seemed to be her own special and peculiar form of beauty. *War and Peace, i, 1*

Never marry till you can say to yourself that you have done all you are capable of, and until you have ceased to love the woman of your choice and have seen her plainly as she is, or else you will make a cruel and irrevocable mistake. *Ibid., i, 2*

Tie yourself up with a woman, and like a chained convict you lose all freedom! And all you have of hope and strength merely weighs you down and torments you with regret. *Ibid.*

... the endless variety of men's minds, which prevents a truth from ever presenting itself identically to two persons. *Ibid., vi, 3*

... one of those men who choose their opinions like their clothes, according to the fashion, but who for that reason appear to be the warmest partisans. *Ibid., vi, 10*

The less attractive a woman is the more constant she is likely to be. *Ibid., vi, 12*

He could not comprehend how any one could wish to alter his life or introduce anything new into it, when his own life was already ending. *Ibid., vi, 14*

Berg, judging by his wife, thought all women weak and foolish. Vera, judging by her husband and generalizing from that observation, supposed that all men, though they understand nothing and are conceited and selfish, ascribe common sense to themselves alone.

Ibid.

Countess Bezukhova quite deserved her reputation for being a fascinating woman. She could say what she did not think – especially what was flattering – quite simply and naturally. *Ibid.*, viii, 9

Marshal Dâvot was one of those men who purposely put themselves in most depressing conditions to have a justification for being gloomy. *Ibid.*, ix, 5

A man who does not know Paris is a savage.

Ibid., xi, 14

All happy families resemble one another, but each unhappy family is unhappy in its own way.

Anna Karenina

Woman ... is such a subject that however much you study it, it is always new. *Ibid.*

By prudent marriages we mean those in which both parties have sown their wild oats already.

Ibid.

Before, when I was told to consider him clever, I kept looking for his ability, and thought myself a fool for not seeing it; but directly I said 'He's a fool', though only in a whisper, everything was explained. *Ibid.*

In getting to know thoroughly one's wife, if one loves her ... one gets to know all women better than if one knew thousands of them. *Ibid.*

With friends, one is well; but at home, one is better.

Ibid.

For him all the girls in the world were divided into two classes: one class – all the girls in the world except her, and those girls had all sorts of human weaknesses and were very ordinary; the other class – she alone, having no weaknesses of any sort and higher than all humanity.

Ibid.

A wife is a care, but it's worse when she's not a wife.

Ibid.

In order to carry through any undertaking in family life, there must necessarily be either complete division between husband and wife, or loving agreement. When the relations of a couple are vacillating and neither one thing nor the other, no sort of enterprise can be undertaken.

Ibid.

He was the familiar friend of everyone with whom he took a glass of champagne, and he took a glass of champagne with everyone.

Ibid.

He had heard that women often did care for ugly and ordinary men, but he did not believe it, for he judged by himself, and he could not have loved any but beautiful, mysterious and exceptional women.

Ibid.

She was jealous not of any particular woman but of the decrease of his love. Not having an object for her jealousy, she was on the lookout for one.

Ibid.

As is not infrequent with women of unimpeachable virtue, weary of the monotony of respectable existence, at a distance she not only excused illicit love but positively envied it.

Ibid.

He had a code of principles which defined with unfailing certitude what he ought and ought not to do … that one must pay a cardsharper, but need not pay a tailor; that one must never tell a lie to a man, but one may to a woman; that one must never cheat anyone, but one may a husband; that one must never pardon an insult, but one may give one, and so on.   *Ibid.*

He looked at her as a man looks at a faded flower he has gathered, with difficulty recognising in it the beauty for which he picked and ruined it.

Ibid.

Everything she did for him was entirely for her own sake, and she told him she was doing it for herself, as if that was so incredible that he must understand the opposite.   *Ivan Ilyich and Hadji Murad*

Real debauchery lies precisely in freeing oneself from moral relations with a woman with whom you have physical intimacy.

The Kreutzer Sonata

If a one-hundredth part of the efforts devoted to the cure of syphilis were devoted to the eradication of debauchery, there would long ago not have been a trace of syphilis left.

Ibid.

As a morphinist, a drunkard, or a smoker is no longer normal, so too a man who has known several women for his pleasure is not normal but is a man perverted for ever, a libertine.

Ibid.

Ask any expert coquette who has set herself the task of captivating a man, which she would prefer to risk: to be convicted in his presence of lying, of cruelty, or even of dissoluteness, or to appear before him in an ugly and badly made dress – she will always prefer the first.

Ibid.

Prostitutes for short terms are usually despised, while prostitutes for long terms are respected.

Ibid.

Our stimulating super abundance of food, together with complete physical idleness, is nothing but a systematic excitement of lust.

Ibid.

'Aha, you just want us to be the objects of your sensuality, do you? All right, then, it's as the objects of your sensuality that we'll enslave you,' say women.

Ibid.

See what it is that everywhere impedes the forward movement of mankind. Women!

Ibid.

The education of women will always correspond to men's opinions about them.

Ibid.

A woman is happy and attains all she can desire when she has bewitched a man. Therefore the chief aim of a woman is to be able to bewitch him. So it has been and will be.

Ibid.

Children are a torment and nothing else. Most mothers feel this quite plainly, and sometimes inadvertently say so.

Ibid.

Our relations to one another grew more and more hostile and at last reached a stage where it was not disagreement that caused hostility but hostility that caused disagreement. Whatever she might say I disagreed with beforehand.

Ibid.

I was convinced that I knew just what he would say and do, and how he would look; and if anything he did surprised me, I concluded that he had made a mistake. I expected nothing from him. In a word, he was my husband.

Ibid.

Every woman, however she may dress herself and however she may call herself and however refined she may be, who refrains from childbirth without refraining from sexual relations, is a whore.

What Then Must We Do?

It is women who form public opinion.

Ibid.

Without women doctors, women telegraphists, women lawyers and scientists and authoresses, we might get on, but without mothers, helpers, friends, comforters, who love in man all that is best in him – without such women it would be hard to live in the world.

What Is Art?

The business of a woman, by her very vocation, is different from that of a man. And therefore the ideal of perfection for a woman cannot be the same as the ideal for a man.

Ibid.

Marriage, far from being a happiness, is always a misery – the price of sexual satisfaction.

Life of Tolstoy

One's family is one's flesh.

Ibid.

Man survives earthquakes, epidemics, terrible illnesses, and every kind of spiritual suffering, but always the most poignant tragedy was, is, and ever will be the tragedy of the bedroom.

Ibid.

I've been lowering my opinion of women for seventy years, but I need to lower it still further.

Ibid.

Politics

Influence in society ... is capital which has to be economized.
War and Peace, i, 1

A Frenchman is self-assured because he regards himself personally both in mind and body as irresistibly attractive to men and women. An Englishman is self-assured as being a citizen of the best-organized state in the world and therefore, as an Englishman, always knows what he should do and knows that all he does as an Englishman is undoubtedly correct. An Italian is self-assured because he is excitable and easily forgets himself and other people. A Russian is self-assured just because he knows nothing and does not want to know anything, since he does not believe that anything can be known. The German's self-assurance is worst of all, because he imagines that he knows the truth – science – which he himself has invented but which is for him the absolute truth.
Ibid., ix, 10

The chief way to make people obey is to show no suspicion that they can possibly disobey.
Ibid., x, 9

Every Russian looking at Moscow feels her to be a mother; every foreigner who sees her, even if ignorant of her significance as the mother city, must feel her feminine character.
Ibid., xi, 10

Since the world began and men have killed one another no one ever committed a crime against his fellow-man without comforting himself with this idea. This idea is *le bien public*, the hypothetical welfare of other people. To a man not swayed by passion, that welfare is never certain, but he who commits such a crime always knows just where that welfare lies.
Ibid., xi, 12

One need only admit that public tranquillity is in danger and any action finds a justification. All the horrors of the Reign of Terror were based only on solicitude for public tranquillity. *Ibid.*

In quiet and untroubled times it seems to every administrator that it is only by his efforts that the whole population under his rule is kept going, and in this consciousness of being indispensable every administrator finds the chief reward of his labour.

Ibid.

Power is power: in other words, power is a word the meaning of which we do not understand.

Ibid., EP.II

What is called power over others is in its real meaning only the greatest dependence on them.

Ibid.

A secretary came in, with respectful familiarity and the modest consciousness, characteristic of every secretary, of being superior to his chief in the knowledge of their business. *Anna Karenina*

He's persecuted by the police, of course, because he's not a scoundrel. *Ibid.*

Being poor does not deprive men of reason. They never have admitted and never will admit that it is right for some to have a perpetual holiday while others must always fast and work ... Where there is a man not working because he is able to compel others to work for him – there slavery exists.

What Then Must We Do?

I sit on a man's back, choking him and making him carry me, and yet assure myself and others that I am very sorry for him and wish to ease his lot by all possible means – except by getting off his back.

Ibid.

Formerly men took the labour of others simply by violence – slavery. Today we do it by property.

Ibid.

Power is always seized by those who are less conscientious and less moral.

Kingdom of God and Peace Essays

One of two things: either people are rational beings or they are irrational beings. If they are irrational beings, then they are all irrational, and then everything among them is decided by violence, and there is no reason why certain people should, and others should not, have a *right* to use violence. And in that case governmental violence has no justification. But if men are rational beings, then their relations should be based on reason, and not on the violence of those who happen to have seized power. And in that case, again, governmental violence has no justification.

Ibid.

The organization of government is unimaginable without murders and is therefore incompatible with Christianity.

Recollections and Essays

Society resembles a crystal. No matter how you grind it, dissolve it, compress it, it will reform itself at the first opportunity into the same form.

Life of Tolstoy

Socialists will never destroy poverty and the inequality of capacities ... Even if Marx's predictions take place, the only thing that will happen is that a new despotism will be passed on.

Ibid.

'Property is theft' will remain more truthful than the British constitution so long as mankind exists.

Ibid.

There is no such thing as political change of the social system: there is only moral change within men and women.

Ibid.

The worst thing is a compromise accepted as a principle.

Ibid.

One can't use more than a certain amount of that which is necessary, but to luxury there are no bounds ... Hence no increase in wealth will improve the lot of the lower classes while the upper classes have the power to spend all they desire on luxuries.

Ibid.

People write pompously that where there are rights there are also obligations ... But man has only obligations.

Ibid.

My anarchism is simply the application of Christianity to human affairs.

Ibid.

Personal egoism is a minor evil, family egoism is bigger, and party egoism is bigger still; but state egoism is the worst of all.

Ibid.

Himself

In the course of my life, I have never met a man who was all bad, all pride, all good or all intelligence ... I see stupidity in the most intelligent book, intelligent things in the conversation of the greatest fool alive.

Childhood, Boyhood, and Youth

The hero of my tale – whom I love with all the power of my soul, whom I have tried to portray in all his beauty, who has been, is, and will be, beautiful – is Truth.

Tales of Army Life

I could gain much in life if I were willing to work without conviction.

Ibid.

As long as I have any superfluous food and someone else has none, and I have two coats and someone else has none, I share in a constantly repeated crime.

What Then Must We Do?

If I wish to help others I must first of all cease causing suffering.

Ibid.

I departed for the country, vexed with others – as is always the case – because I had myself done something stupid and bad.

Ibid.

I am a quite enfeebled, good-for-nothing parasite, who can only exist under most exceptional conditions found only when thousands of people labour to support a life that is of no value to anyone.

Ibid.

I found intercourse with this kind of unfortunates particularly trying, and I now understand why. In them I saw myself as in a looking-glass.

Ibid.

Thirty years ago in Paris I once saw how, in the presence of thousands of spectators, they cut a man's head off with a guillotine. I knew that the man was a dreadful criminal ... but at the moment the head and body separated and fell into the box I gasped, and realized not with my mind nor with my heart but with my whole being, that all arguments in defence of capital punishment are wicked nonsense.

Ibid.

I often have to make an effort to restrain myself from desiring the death of the body.

On Life and Essays on Religion

I believe every good action increases the true welfare of my eternal life and every evil action decreases it.

Ibid.

In the periodical absolution of sins at Confession I see a harmful deception which only encourages immorality and causes men not to fear sin.

Ibid.

I consider all the Sacraments to be coarse, degrading sorcery, incompatible with the idea of God or with the Christian teaching.

Ibid.

I began by loving my Orthodox faith more than my peace, then I loved Christianity more than my Church, and now I love truth more than anything in the world.

Ibid.

I believe in this: I believe in God, whom I understand as Spirit, as Love, as the source of all. I believe he is in me and I in him ... I believe therefore that the meaning of the life of every man is to be found only in increasing the love that is in him; that this increase of love leads man, even in this life, to ever greater and greater blessedness, and after death gives him the more blessedness the more love he has.
Ibid.

Whether or not these beliefs of mine offend, grieve, or prove a stumbling-block to anyone, or hinder anything, or give displeasure to anybody, I can as little change them as I can change my body.
Ibid.

Looking back on that time, I now see clearly that my faith – my only real faith – that which apart from my animal instincts gave impulse to my life – was a belief in perfecting myself.
A Confession

Every time I tried to express my most sincere desire, which was to be morally good, I met with contempt and ridicule, but as soon as I yielded to low passions I was praised and encouraged.
Ibid.

Someone had played an evil and stupid joke on me by placing me in the world.
Ibid.

Lying, robbery, adultery of all kinds, drunkenness, violence, murder – there was no crime I did not commit, and in spite of that people praised my conduct and my contemporaries considered me to be a comparatively moral man.
Ibid.

I lived as a parasite, and on asking myself, what is the use of my life? I got the reply: 'No use.'
Ibid.

As long as I did not know why, I could do nothing and could not live.

Ibid.

I understood that it was not an error in my thought that had hid the truth from me so much as my life itself in the exceptional conditions of epicurean gratification of desire in which I passed it.

Ibid.

I perceived that to understand the meaning of life it is necessary first that life should not be meaningless and evil.

Ibid.

I instinctively felt that if I wished to live and understand the meaning of life, I must seek this meaning not among those who have lost it and wish to kill themselves, but among those milliards of the past and the present who make life and support the burden of their own lives and ours also … the simple labouring folk.

Ibid.

My question – that which at the age of fifty brought me to the verge of suicide – was the simplest of questions, lying in the soul of every man from the foolish child to the wisest elder: it was a question without an answer to which one cannot live, as I had found from experience. It was: 'What will come of what I am doing today or shall do tomorrow? What will come of my whole life?'

Ibid.

I sought painfully and long, not from idle curiosity or listlessly, but painfully and persistently day and night – sought as a perishing man seeks for safety – and I found nothing.

Ibid.

I did not understand life. It seemed to me terrible. And suddenly I heard the words of Christ and understood them, and life and death ceased to seem to me evil, and instead of despair I experienced happiness and the joy of life undisturbed by death.

Ibid.

The arbiter of what is good and evil is not what people say and do, nor is it progress, but it is my heart and I.

Ibid.

People often express regret that man's memory will not survive death. But how fortunate that it does not! What torture it would be if I in a future life remembered all the bad things I have done in this life and that now torment my conscience. *Recollections and Essays*

Capital punishment has been and remains for me one of those human actions the actual performance of which does not infringe in me the consciousness of their impossibility. I understand that under the influence of momentary irritation, hatred, revenge, or loss of consciousness of his humanity, a man may kill another in his own defence or in defence of a friend; or that under the influence of patriotic mass-hypnotism and while exposing himself to death he may take part in collective murder in war. But that men in full control of their human attributes can quietly and deliberately admit the necessity of killing a fellow man, and can oblige others to perform that action so contrary to human nature, I never can understand.

Ibid.

There is something in me which forces me to think that I was not born to be what other men are.

Diary

I lack all modesty! That is my main defect.

Ibid.

Must grow accustomed to no one ever understanding me. It must be a fate common to all men who are difficult to get on with.

Ibid.

It is good that I am ashamed of myself, but I must not take pride in this fact.

Ibid.

From my youth onward I always admired more than anything else that negative quality – simplicity.

Life of Tolstoy

At times the truth passed through me, and these were the happiest moments of my life.

Ibid.

It is as though I alone were not mad in a house of lunatics managed by lunatics.

Ibid.

I used to believe that there was a green stick, buried on the edge of a ravine in the old Zakaz forest at Yasnaya Polyana, on which words were carved that would destroy all the evil in the hearts of men and bring them everything good.

Ibid.

Ars longa, vita brevis. Sometimes I am sorry. There is so much I wish to say.

Ibid.

I know that I am both evil and stupid, and yet people consider me to be a man of genius. So what must other people be like?

Ibid.

I can't understand why God chose such a repulsive
creature as I through which to speak to people.

Ibid.

I did not become a general in the army, but I did in
literature.

Ibid.

Art

This is the strange fate of art ... All seek it and love it – it is the one thing everybody wants and tries to find in life, yet nobody acknowledges its power, nobody values this greatest blessing in the world, nor esteems or is grateful to those who give it to mankind.

The Snow Storm

Why speak, when words cannot express what one feels?

War and Peace, vi, 14

... the simplest, clearest, and therefore most terrible thoughts.

Ibid., x, 24

Plump self-satisfied thinkers and artists, enjoying themselves, do not exist.

What Then Must We Do?

The essence of art consists in the infection of the contemplator of a work by the author's feelings.

Recollections and Essays

Shakespeare may be anything you like – only not an artist.

Ibid.

I think Shakespeare cannot be admitted to be either a writer of great genius or even an average one.

Ibid.

All of Shakespeare's characters speak not a language of their own but always one and the same Shakespearian, affected, unnatural language, which not only could they not speak, but which no real people could ever have spoken anywhere.

Ibid.

A writer is precious and necessary for us only to the extent to which he reveals to us the inner labour of his soul.

What Is Art?

Art is not handicraft, it is the transmission of feeling the artist has experienced.

Ibid.

A true work of art is the revelation (by laws beyond our grasp) of a new conception of life arising in the artist's soul, which, when expressed, lights up the path along which humanity progresses.

Ibid.

An artist is an artist because he sees things not as he wishes to see them but as they really are.

Ibid.

The ballet, in which half-naked women make voluptuous movements, twisting themselves into various sensual wreathings, is simply a lewd performance.

Ibid.

To see the aim and purpose of art in the pleasure we get from it, is like assuming ... that the purpose and aim of food is the pleasure derived when consuming it.

Ibid.

Though a work of art must always include something new, yet the revelation of something new will not always be a work of art.

Ibid.

If a man is infected by the author's condition of soul, if he feels this emotion and this union with others, then the object which has effected this is art ... And not only is this infection a sure sign of art, but the degree of infection is also the sole measure of excellence in art.

Ibid.

If only it be admitted that art may be unintelligible to any one of sound mind and yet be art, there is no reason why any circle of perverted people should not compose works tickling their own perverted feelings and comprehensible to no one but themselves, and call it 'art'.

Ibid.

Printing, which is undoubtedly useful for the great masses of uneducated people, among well-to-do people has long become the chief organ for the dissemination of ignorance, and not of enlightenment.

Ibid.

If in our day a clever young man of the people wishing to educate himself, is given access to all books, periodicals, and newspapers, and the choice of his reading is left to himself, he will, if he reads for ten years assiduously every day, in all probability read nothing but stupid and immoral books.

Ibid.

The immoral, coarse, inflated, disconnected babble of Nietzsche ...

Ibid.

In all the theatres plays are produced the meaning of which is unknown to any one, even to the authors, and novels that have no content and no artistic merit are printed and circulated by millions under the guise of artistic productions.   *Ibid.*

To be good, literary compositions must be ... sung from the soul of the author.

Life of Tolstoy

You can invent anything you please, but you cannot invent psychology.

Ibid.

A human life is more precious than any piece of writing.

Ibid.